ENVIRONMENT

Written by
Keith Bishop

Illustrated by
Maltings Partnership, Satchel Illustration and Cathy Morley

Edited by
Debbie Reid

Designed by
Sarah Peden

Picture research by
Emma Segal

CONTENTS

The global environment	2		Reduce, reuse, recycle	26
Agenda 21	4		Fresh water	28
Sustainable living	6		Seaworld	30
Global links	8		Tourism	32
The global greenhouse	10		Transport today	34
Acid rain	12		Transport tomorrow	36
Holes in the sky	14		Coal, gas and oil	38
Rainforests	16		Alternative energy	40
Endangered species	18		Action taking	42
Deserting the Earth	20		The future?	44
Mountains of waste	22		Glossary	46
Radioactive waste	24		Index	48

The global environment

This book is about the environment – the environment we share with other people and with millions of different species of plants and animals. It explores how we change and damage the environment as a result of our actions.

There are many problems that are endangering the future of this planet. Most of these problems are linked with one another. However, people have different opinions about how science can help us solve them.

The highlighted words on these pages will give you a guide to these links. Turn to the glossary on page 46 to see what they mean. This will help you to see some of the major environmental issues and how they are linked.

The Sun – sunlight and warmth travelling 150 million km is the source of energy for life on Earth.

Biosphere
This is the living land, air and water around the Earth which supports plant and animal life.

Global warming
This is a problem of too much carbon dioxide and other **greenhouse gases**. These gases cause too much of the Sun's energy to be trapped in the biosphere.

Acid rain
Fossil fuels release toxic gases that cause **acid rain** when they are burnt to make electricity.

Alternative energy sources
These offer other ways of making electricity, but they have their problems.

Holes in the sky
The **ozone layer** is a natural filter that blocks out most of the dangerous ultra-violet rays from the Sun. The man-made **CFCs** that destroy the ozone layer are also greenhouse gases.

Rainforests
The rainforests pump oxygen into the biosphere and also reduce the amount of carbon dioxide. Cutting down and burning the forests simply increases the level of greenhouse gases and that leads to **global warming**.

Endangered species
Fifty per cent of the world's species of plants and animals live in the rainforests. If we destroy the rainforests, we reduce the natural **biodiversity** of the planet.

Stratosphere
Troposphere
The Earth

Deserting the Earth
Deforestation and over-grazing take away the soil's natural protective layer of plants. The result is poor quality soil. This process is called **desertification**.

Mountains of waste
Non-renewable resources are wasted to produce rubbish which then **pollutes** the environment. Tipping rubbish in landfill sites or burning it produces greenhouse gases, and **pollutes** the water supply.

Radioactive waste
This does not give off greenhouse gases or gases that cause acid rain. However, radioactive waste is a long term pollutant which nobody wants and which is difficult to get rid of.

Fresh water
Global warming could be affecting the pattern of rainfall around the globe. **Pollution** of the water supply is caused by sewage and **toxins** from domestic waste.

Seaworld
Toxins and other pollutants from industry damage the **food chains** in the sea.

Transport today
Transport is using up non-renewable resources and polluting the atmosphere with greenhouse gases and other toxins.

Transport tomorrow
Transport of the future will have a major impact on global warming and the health of the environment.

4 Agenda 21

In June 1992, in Rio de Janeiro, 35 000 people attended the biggest conference ever held in the world – the Earth Summit. Representatives from 178 countries were there to talk about the environment. It produced a report called Agenda 21 which presented 115 proposals about sustainable living from now into the 21st Century.

Children with 'The tree of life' at the Earth Summit, Rio de Janeiro, Brazil

The Earth Summit also produced two important agreements about climate change and biodiversity.

1 Climate change

This says that, by the year 2000, emissions of carbon dioxide and other greenhouse gases must be cut back to 1990 levels.

2 Biodiversity

This aims to protect plant and animal species all over the world before it's too late.

These two agreements might seem simple enough, but actually achieving them is not going to be so easy. If we are going to have an environment healthy enough to sustain future generations, then governments must agree to act now.

What did the Earth Summit achieve?

The Earth Summit brought people from all over the world to talk together. They produced Agenda 21 – a 600 billion dollar action programme to save the planet. Agenda 21 asks how you want to see the planet being treated and what kind of future you want to see for your children and grandchildren. Most of Agenda 21 says what governments can do, but there is a chapter aimed at young people and how important their involvement is.

Local Agenda 21

Agenda 21 can can only work if people act locally. Local Agenda 21 is your chance to be involved in environmental action and find ways to 'be more sustainable' in your local area.

In England and Wales, every local council is expected to organise a Local Agenda 21 to bring people together to act on environmental issues. Most councils have a Environmental Services Department which deals with environmental issues such as conservation or recycling.

How can I be involved?

You can find out what is going on in your area by ringing the council number and asking for information about Local Agenda 21. Solutions to local problems can have a knock-on effect which will improve the global environment. Local Agenda 21 will help you make those links between local and global problems.

Local Agenda 21 can put you in touch with community groups and help you to meet other people who want to do something for their environment. If there aren't any groups, then it could help you form groups and advise you what to do.

They may also be able to provide some funds to help you get started when you know what you want to do.

What can we do?

Here are some ideas for Local Agenda 21 action:

■ Find out how you could help to reduce traffic pollution in your area.

■ Develop a community composting project.

■ Repair local footpaths.

■ Increase biodiversity. Develop green spaces as conservation areas.

■ Clean up a local pond or stream. Set up a study to find out where the pollution is coming from.

■ Write to your local MP about any issues that concern you.

Local Agenda 21 is about meeting other people in your community to take action on the environment.

Dog mess bins encourage people to keep their environment clean and safe.

6 Sustainable living

Sustainable living is about caring for the Earth and its systems for supporting life. It's about whether we can go on damaging the environment for future generations by using up the Earth's resources and polluting the environment with waste.

Have you ever thought about all the rubbish that's left at the end of a party? Someone comes round and sweeps all the the clingfilm, plastic cups, spoons, knives, forks and paper plates into a big, black, plastic bin liner. Think about how long this material was used for before it was thrown away. Where did it all come from, and where is it all going to end up?

The plastics all come from oil which is a non-renewable resource. When it's used up, it can't be replaced. Why do we treat the Earth's resources in this way? We use them up when we make things, only to throw them away again almost as quickly.

Are we misusing our natural resources by always making 'throwaway' things? In other words, is our style of living sustainable? Will there still be enough resources left for future generations?

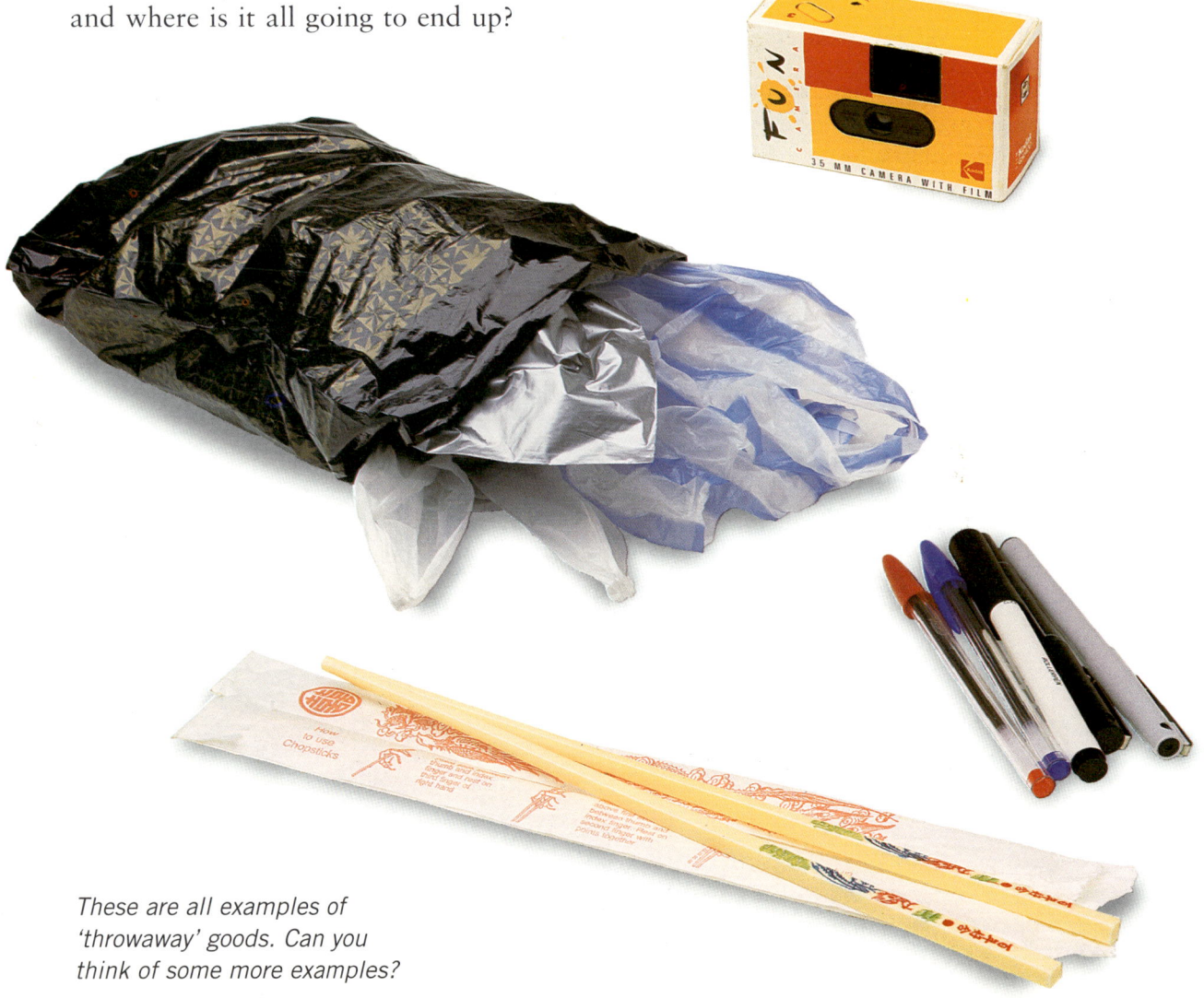

These are all examples of 'throwaway' goods. Can you think of some more examples?

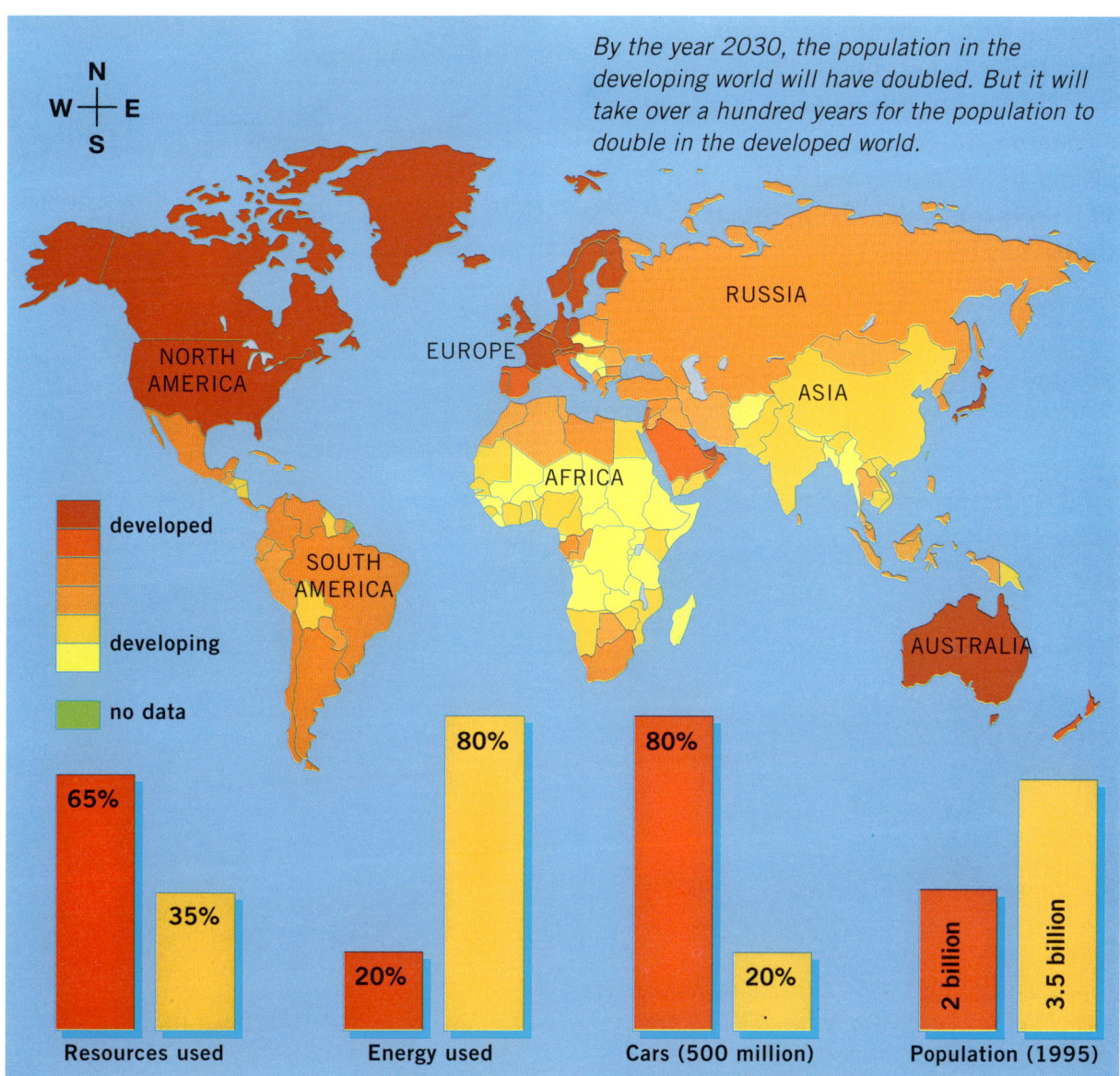

Who's using up the resources?

The developed world has a quarter of the world's population, but it uses up twice the amount of resources as the other three quarters (see map above).

Look at the map and work out roughly what the world population could be by the year 2030. Where do you think most of the new people on the planet will be living?

Damaging the environment

High living standards means using the Earth's resources to make consumer goods like toys, cars, televisions and washing machines. But making the goods, as well as using them and then throwing them away, creates waste. And waste can cause pollution which damages the environment.

Think about what will happen to the environment if everyone lives this way.

8 Global links

Human beings do not live separately from other living things. We are all linked together through our common environment. Actions we take in our corner of the globe could affect the lives of people and other living things thousands of miles away.

CFCs destroy the ozone layer high in the atmosphere.

Growing cash crops, such as peanuts, reduces the amount of land available for people to graze their animals and grow their own food.

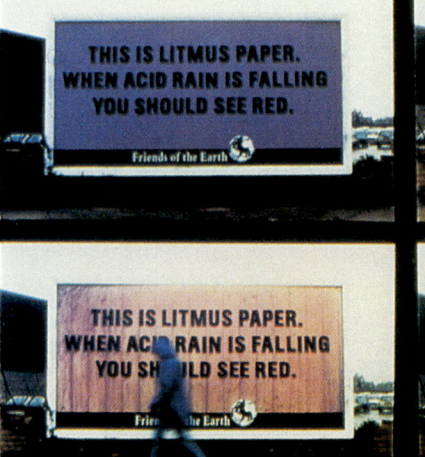

Acid rain is pollution which falls wherever the wind blows it.

Doctors claim that traffic fumes increase the chances of children becoming asthmatic.

Endangered species are threatened by people who want to buy their skins, tusks or other parts of their bodies.

Scientists are sure that increasing carbon dioxide levels are causing the climate to change all round the world.

The global greenhouse

Have you ever walked into a greenhouse on a cool but bright, sunny day? It feels nice and warm. In fact, we all live in a global greenhouse. The Earth's atmosphere acts just like the glass and keeps the warmth in. Without this 'greenhouse effect', life could not exist as we know it. Our worry now is that the Earth is getting a bit too warm, and we're not sure what the consequences might be.

Global warming

This increased greenhouse effect is called global warming. It is caused by too much carbon dioxide in the air. Carbon dioxide is the most important of the greenhouse gases simply because some of us produce so much of it. A person in the United States, for example, causes emissions of carbon dioxide ten times more than someone in Asia.

The highest point on the Maldives Islands is only 160 cm above sea level.

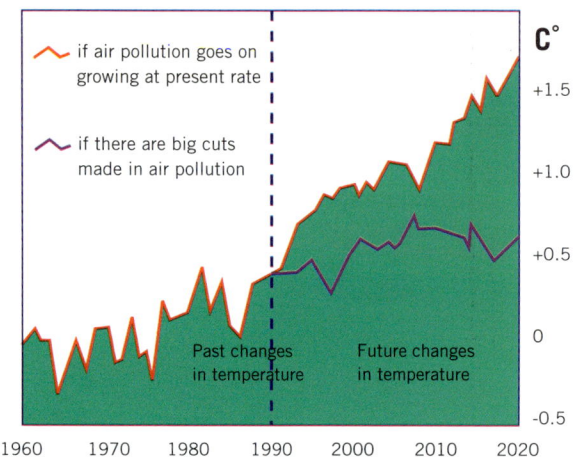

What's the problem?

The average temperature of the sea and the atmosphere is going up. By the year 2030, it could be 1 degree higher. This doesn't seem much, but it could be enough to start melting the polar ice caps. It's estimated that 2.5 thousand square miles of the ice shelf in Antarctica has already disappeared into the sea during the last fifty years. If this is true, the sea level will rise. You may not worry too much about flooding if you live well above sea level, but millions of people don't! Look at the map. The Maldives Islands could disappear under water completely.

We are also worried about changing weather patterns. Many countries already suffer from low rainfall. Global warming could make matters worse by causing even more severe droughts.

Where's all the carbon dioxide coming from?

Industrialised countries burn massive amounts of fossil fuel to make electricity and to provide fuel for transport.

It's estimated that an average British family is responsible for 20 tonnes of carbon dioxide being pumped into the air every year. In the 1990s, this adds up world wide to about 500 billion tonnes a year.

A burning rainforest in the Amazon

Greenhouse gases

Not only do trees use up carbon dioxide when they photosynthesise but when they are burnt (see photo), they release carbon dioxide back into the atmosphere. Unless we replant trees, there will be fewer and fewer to use up the carbon dioxide.

Carbon dioxide isn't the only greenhouse gas that's causing the problem. There are others such as CFCs (see page 14) from fridges, and even methane gas from animal pits on farms!

What can we do?

The Earth Summit (see page 4) produced a very important agreement called the Law on Climate Change. This says that, by the year 2000, countries should reduce their carbon dioxide emissions to the 1990 level. This is a real challenge if developing countries are also going to improve their living standards at the same time.

What can you do? Look at the pictures (below) to give you some ideas of how you can help reduce greenhouse gases.

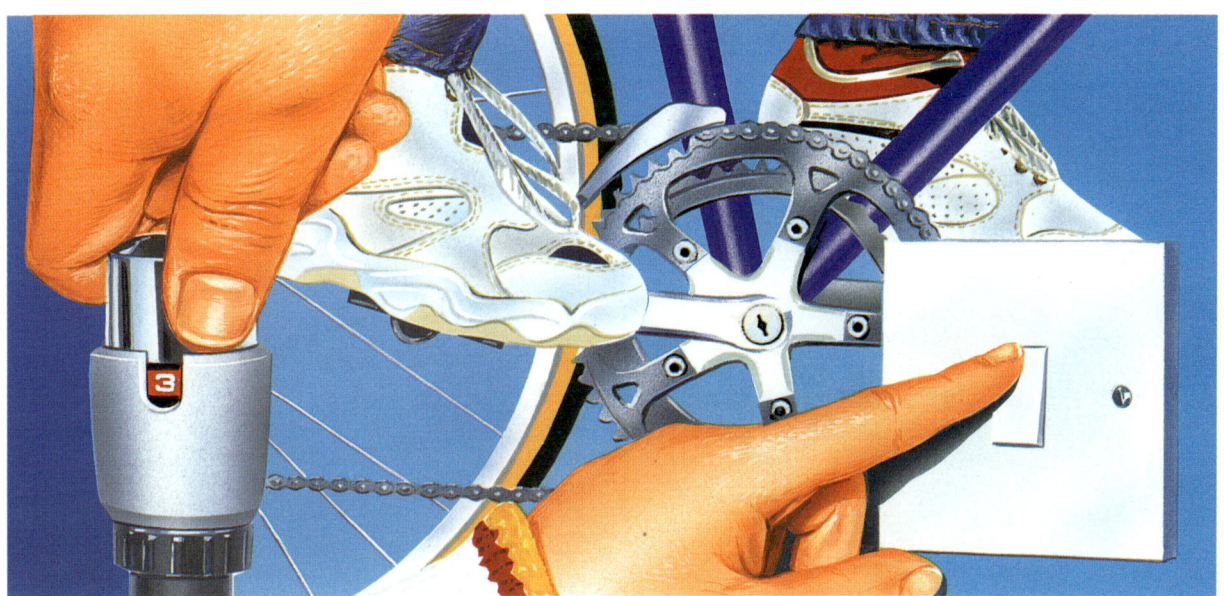

Simple actions can help to reduce greenhouse gases. Every little helps!

Acid rain

Waste gases from power stations, industry and transport rise high into the sky and pollute the atmosphere. There they travel with the wind, often over vast distances, crossing different countries as they go. The gases dissolve in water in the clouds and fall back to the Earth as acid rain. This causes environmental damage.

All European countries produce acid rain by releasing poisonous gases which pollute the atmosphere. Look at the map. Which countries do you think are going to suffer most from acid rain?

Which gases make acid rain?

There are two main gases: sulphur dioxide (SO_2) and nitrogen oxides (NO_x).

The sulphur dioxide comes mostly from coal-fired power stations and heavy industry. Most of the nitrogen oxides come from the exhaust gases of cars and trucks.

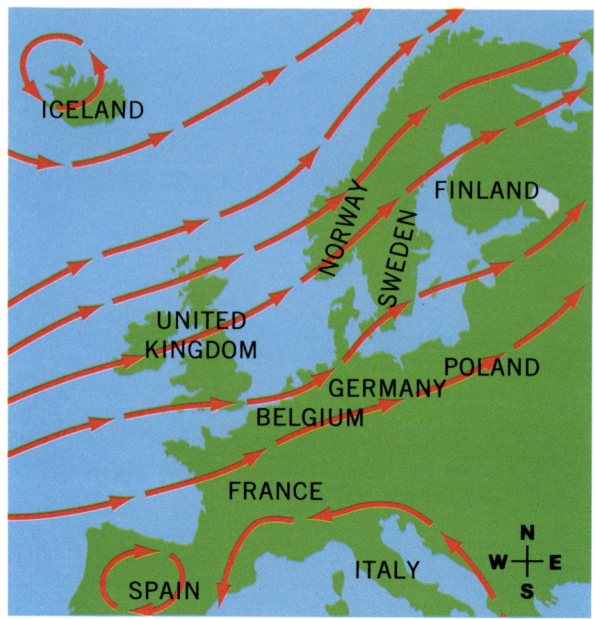

Prevailing winds blow from the south west and take pollution over Scandinavia.

Key
- coal with sulphur impurities
- coal burnt in power station
- SO_2 drifts into atmosphere
- SO_2 combines with water
- acid rain falls to Earth
- exhaust gases containing NO_x and SO_2

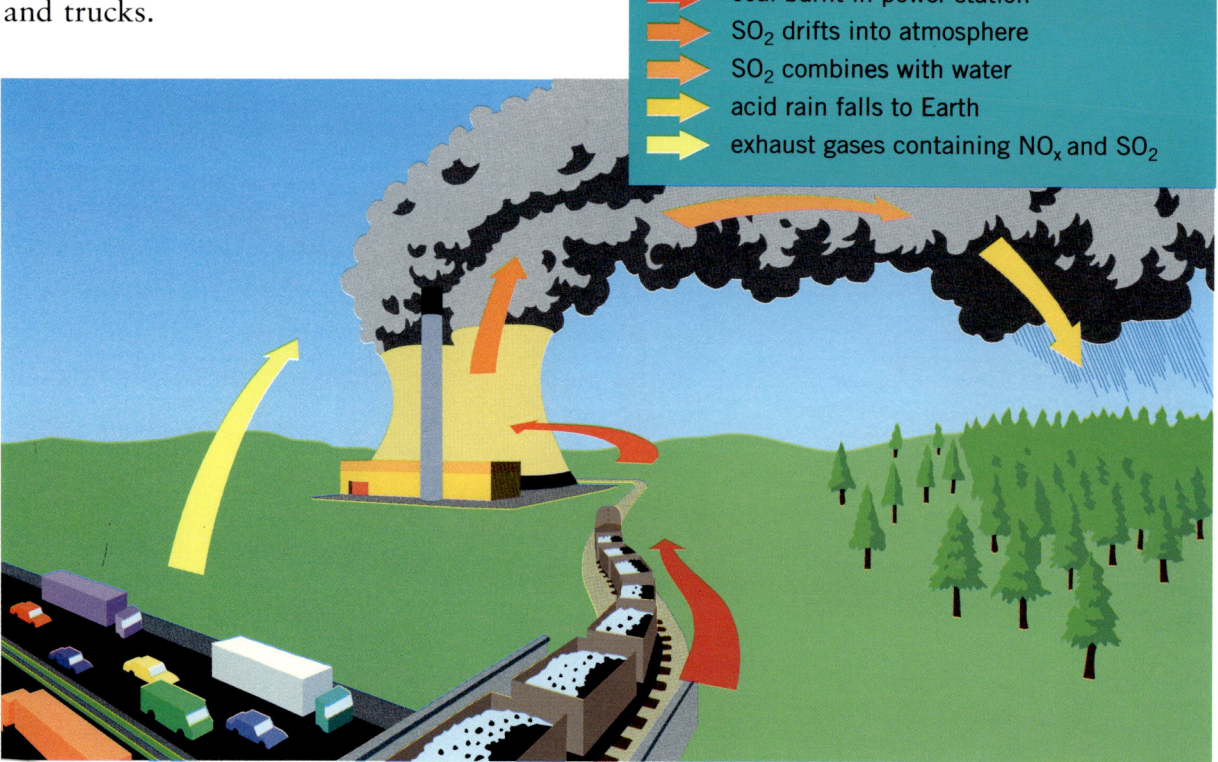

What could be done to reduce the amount of acid rain being formed?

What's the damage?

Acid rain gets into the soil and affects the way trees grow. The branches begin to sag and die back.

Acid rain damage to a statue in Poland. What do you feel about the damage acid rain does?

Many beautiful buildings and statues, particularly those made from limestone or marble, are dissolved away by acid rain (see photo).

Acid rain also pollutes freshwater lakes. Over 40 per cent of Sweden's lakes are now almost lifeless. The photo (below) shows a beautiful, crystal clear lake. If you looked closely, you would see very few plants or fish. This is because the water is too acidic for living things to survive.

The polluter pays

Together, the United States and Europe release over 70 million tons of sulphur dioxide and 40 million tonnes of nitrogen oxides into the atmosphere every year. They are responsible for 80 per cent of the world's acid rain and photochemical smog.

Some people think that if you pollute the environment, then you should pay for the damage you cause. This is called 'the polluter pays' principle. What do you think of this idea?

Lake Gardsjon, Sweden. This lake is polluted by acid rain. Only the very hardiest plants and animals can survive in the water.

What can we do?

Acid rain is a problem that can be controlled. Coal-fired power stations can be fitted with sulphur dioxide removers, but they are expensive.

Another suggestion is that we should build nuclear power stations, or gas-fired power stations instead of burning coal (see page 25).

What can you do? You could help to reduce acid rain pollution by using less electricity and by using the car less often (see pages 37 and 43).

Holes in the sky

High in the sky, over 10 kilometres above the surface, a thin protective blanket of gas surrounds the Earth. This is the ozone layer, a natural sunblock which filters out the Sun's harmful ultra-violet rays. But during the last twenty years, a large hole has been discovered over the South Pole. Fortunately, not many people live below the hole, but if we don't look after the atmosphere it could be dangerous for people living nearby.

The Antarctic ozone hole, 1995 (centre). Scientists say that the hole is getting bigger each year.

CFCs are used to make these products

CFCs

The holes are where the ozone has thinned to almost a third of what it should be. The cause is mainly a group of chemicals, known as CFCs (chlorofluorocarbons). We use these CFCs to make products such as fridges, foam packaging and fire extinguishers.

We used CFCs because we had no idea what damage they would do. No one realised they would drift up into the stratosphere and set off reactions which would break up the ozone into oxygen.

Unless we do something about the release of CFCs into the environment, our fear is that these holes will gradually grow bigger each year.

Dangerous holes

You've probably been warned lots of times about the dangers of sunbathing. People don't realise that the ultra-violet rays damage living cells and this can sometimes cause skin cancer – even ten to twenty years later.

It is important not to expose your skin to the sun for long periods of time. Try to wear a hat and always use lotions with high protection levels (SPF 15–25).

Banning CFCs

In 1987, governments around the world got together in Montreal. They agreed to ban CFCs and other ozone depleting substances (ODSs) by the year 2000. This was called the Montreal Protocol. Since then, industry has been producing a safer alternative called HFCs. Unfortunately some countries are still producing CFCs, and CFCs are still being sold illegally in the United States.

Did you realise over 100 000 people die every year from skin cancer (melanoma)?

What can we do?

The Montreal Protocol is helping to limit the damage, but the use of CFCs must be stopped. We have no idea what the consequences might be for future generations.

What can you do? If you live in a country where CFCs are still used, you can help by checking that any product you buy is 'CFC free'.

If your family buys a new fridge, make sure that the old one is properly recycled. Check with your local council on how to dispose of it safely.

Some fast food companies use polystyrene containers for their products. Write and ask them if these containers were made using CFCs.

Rainforests

Rainforests are hot, steamy environments where the rainfall can reach 200 mm in a year. They are rich in a wonderful variety of plants and animals, many of which have yet to be discovered. They are also the source of over a quarter of the Earth's oxygen supply. Agenda 21 says they are disappearing so fast that, at this rate, they could all be gone by the year 2035.

Whose rainforest is it?

The native people who live in the rainforest would say it's theirs. But their governments see the rainforest as a way of earning money quickly.

Native people understand the rainforest in a way that we don't. They have developed a sustainable way of life where they take no more from the forest than the forest can replace.

The Yanomami tribe, Venezuelan rainforest. There are over 300 million tribal people in the world.

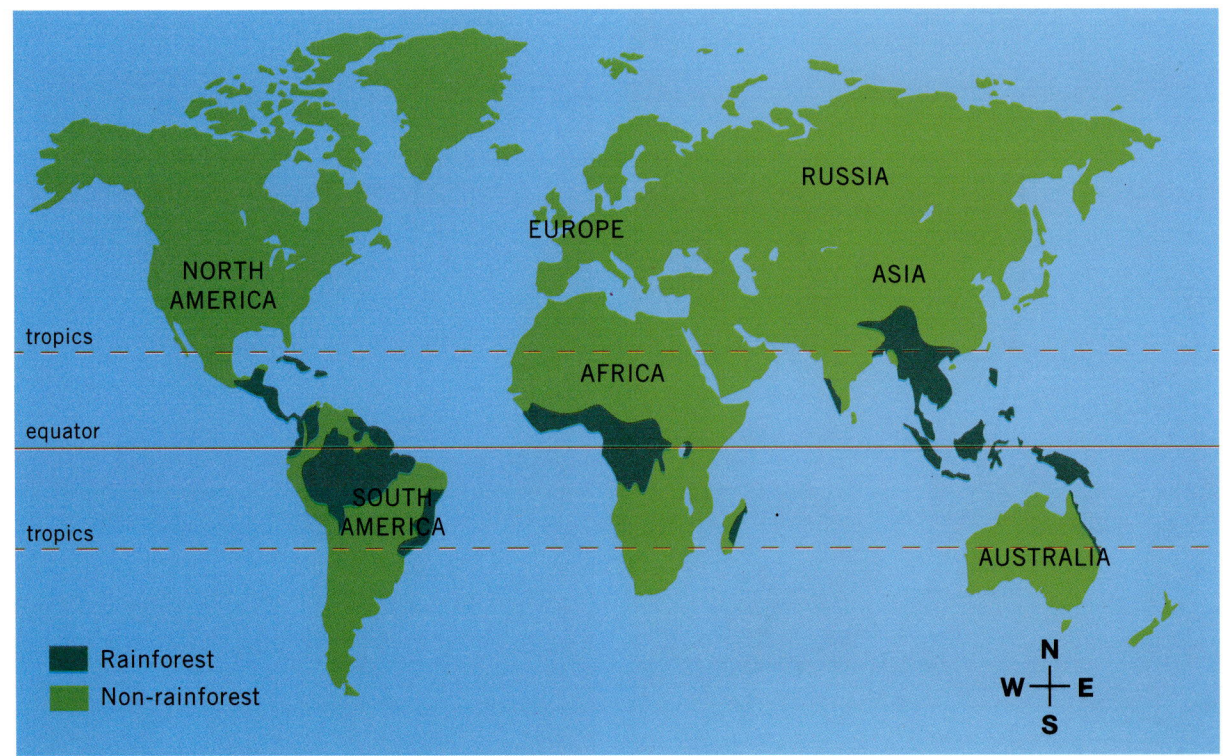

In which parts of the world are rainforests mostly found?

Destroying the rainforest

There are many different reasons for rainforest destruction. The pie chart will help you see how rainforests are being destroyed. The reasons are mostly to do with earning money.

1 Logging destroys most of the forest. Teak, mahogany and ebony are highly prized hardwoods used for making furniture. They take hundreds of years to grow.

2 Ranching also destroys the forest. Much of the beef for burgers in America comes from cattle ranches where there used to be rainforest.

Logging in Queensland, Australia

3 Mining is another reason. Many rainforests are rich in minerals containing silver, copper and gold. Trees are cleared to mine the minerals, leading to soil erosion and landslides. The process of extracting minerals creates terrible pollution of the rivers.

4 Workers from other areas come to work in the rainforest which is burned and cleared to build homes. Few of these workers are the native people.

Twenty years ago, Australia had 200 000 square miles of rainforest. Today, this is down to 60 000 square miles. Logging is the major industry in the rainforest. If developed countries won't set an example, why should developing countries save their rainforests?

Why does burning the forest down add to the problem of global warming?

What can we do?

The Earth Summit produced an important agreement about biodiversity. It talks about preserving the variety of life on this planet. Agenda 21 says we should try to replant trees wherever we can.

What can you do? Ask DIY stores where they get their hardwoods. Some have already agreed not to trade in mahogany.

Think about where the beef for your kingsize burgers comes from.

Endangered species

Every day, it is estimated that fifty species of plants and animals are lost from this planet. Many others are coming close to extinction. We call these the endangered species and they include some of the big mammals such as the black rhinoceros and the mountain gorilla. A report from the United Nations says that 25 per cent of all species could be extinct by the middle of the 21st century.

Human survival depends on the existence and survival of millions of other species. Through our thoughtless actions, we are endangering other species and steadily reducing the biodiversity on this planet.

Becoming extinct

These animals (below) are in danger of becoming extinct (dying out) as they lose their habitats and are hunted for their horns or skins.

The Arabian oryx actually became extinct in the wild in 1972. Some zoos have managed to breed this animal in captivity and have since reintroduced it into the wild.

Trading in endangered species

Birds The photo shows the Spix-macaw, a species like a parrot from the Amazon rainforest in Brazil. This bird is rapidly disappearing from the rainforests. It is sold illegally for up to £5000.

Bears Five of the eight species of bear are in danger. Some people believe that eating certain parts of the bear can help prevent them getting heart or liver disease.

Rhinoceros/elephants The rhinoceros horn is thought to have special medicinal powers by some people in Asia. Poachers make a living by killing animals and selling their tusks and horns. Other people make ornaments and jewellery from the ivory.

Why do you think the Spix-macaw is rapidly disappearing from the rainforests?

As the human population grows people clear the forest, build homes and plant crops. Many endangered plants and animals are being squeezed into smaller and smaller areas where their habitat is still untouched.

Poachers' ivory being burned in Nairobi

What can we do?

Agenda 21 says we should protect the biodiversity of this planet. But we shoot animals for their skins, furs, horns and tusks, we force them out of their natural habitats and we pollute their environment.

CITES is the Convention on International Trade in Endangered Species which regulates the world-wide trade in threatened animals and plants. This is action taking at a global level.

What can you do? You could join an organisation such as WWF-UK, which helps conserve animals, plants and habitats for the benefit of all life on Earth.

Deserting the Earth

During the 1980s, about 3 million people around the world died through poverty and starvation. Many of these people were trying to live from a land where the soil was too poor to support their crops or cattle. Through over-grazing, less rainfall and deforestation, the land had been turned into a kind of desert. This is called desertification. Today, it is estimated that a quarter of the surface of the Earth is at risk from desertification.

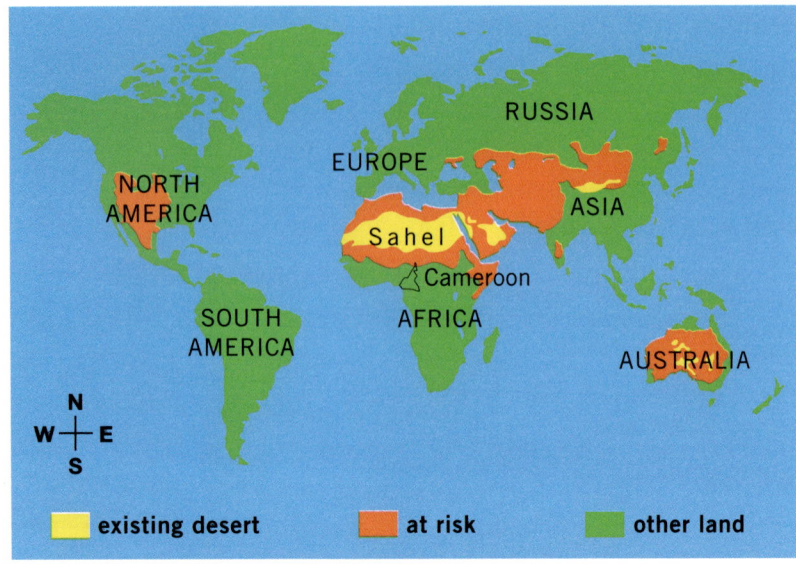

More than a billion people are affected by desertification. Which countries are most affected, and where are they?

Damaging the land

Look at the two photos below. They show how we can spoil the environment.

In the first photo, the land is well covered in vegetation. It can sustain (provide food for) the local nomadic people who roam from place to place. As long as they don't stay too long before finding fresh grazing for their cattle, the land will have time to recover before they come back again.

The second photo shows a very damaged environment. The vegetation is gone and

This land can sustain nomadic people and their cattle.

Cutting down trees and overgrazing the vegetation has exposed the soil to erosion.

the land can't sustain the people any more. In order to survive, the people have had no choice but to cut down the trees for firewood and to let their cattle over-graze the vegetation.

Good land becomes poor land when it is over-grazed and deforested and there is little rainfall. The soil has lost its fertility and cannot support plant life. Any water soon evaporates and the soil becomes dry and loose. The wind then blows it away. This is called erosion.

Harvesting cotton in Vina Valley, Cameroon. Cotton is a 'cash crop'.

Why is this happening?

Why do nomadic people over-graze their land? They usually have no choice. It is often the government which decides how their land is used. If some of their land is taken and used for other purposes, they don't have so much space. So they have to return too quickly to graze the land they have only recently left. In order to live sustainably, they must have the freedom to roam widely across the land.

Cash crops

Have you ever thought about where your packet of peanuts comes from? They could have come from the Sahel. Look at the map on page 20 to see where that is.

Peanuts are often grown on land in the Sahel which used to be traditional nomadic grazing land. They are grown to earn money. This is why they are called 'cash crops'.

Think about what this means for the nomads. How much land will be left for them?

What can we do?

Agenda 21 points out that poverty, starvation and desertification are all closely linked. What do you think about the rights and wrongs of the solutions suggested below?

■ Cash crops should be banned from areas at risk from desertification.

■ Nomadic people should be prevented from roaming the land and over-grazing it.

■ Local people should be given regular food aid from abroad.

What can you do? You could ask about which other products are grown for cash and where they come from. Some suggestions are tea, coffee, chocolate or soya.

Mountains of waste

The United Kingdom produces about 20 million tonnes of household rubbish every year. Most of it is buried in holes in the ground. But the UK is a small country and most people are not keen on living in an environment with so much buried rubbish. Burning the rubbish is possible, but that too has problems. Why do we produce so much waste in the first place?

Filling holes in the ground

The cheapest way of getting rid of rubbish is to fill up holes in the ground (landfill sites). But there are problems. Toxins (poisons) from the rubbish can seep into the earth and pollute the ground water. Organic rubbish, such as food and garden waste, rots. It is a health hazard and it produces a gas called methane which can cause explosions.

For this reason, most rubbish tips are not suitable for building on. Housing developments have been built on some reclaimed tips, but there have been problems. Great care has to be taken to ensure that the site is decontaminated and that the methane gas can escape through specially built vents.

This is a landfill site in Cheshire. Can you think why it is getting harder to find landfill sites?

Should rubbish be burnt?

About 9 per cent of our household rubbish is incinerated (burnt), but this is expensive, even if the heat is used to make electricity. Burning it also produces greenhouse gases and can release toxins, such as dioxin, into the atmosphere.

What's in the rubbish?

Look at the picture. If you sorted and weighed your rubbish, you could see if it is similar to this.

It's been discovered recently that people are discouraged from sorting different materials for recycling if they only have to put all their rubbish in a large wheelie bin.

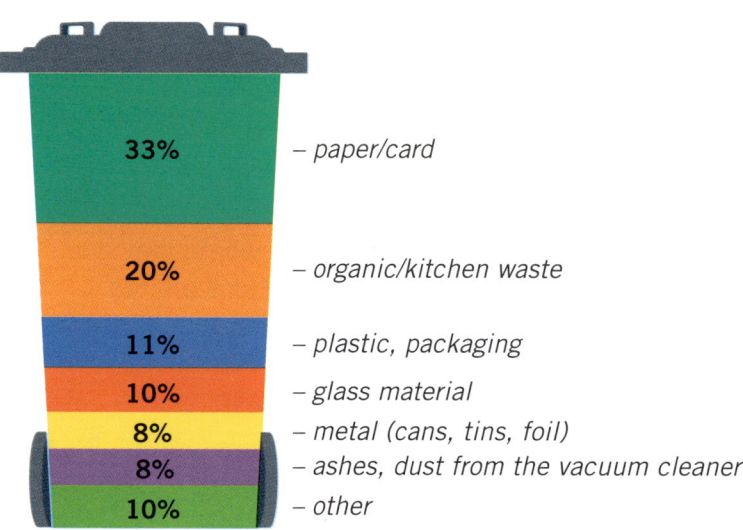

- 33% – paper/card
- 20% – organic/kitchen waste
- 11% – plastic, packaging
- 10% – glass material
- 8% – metal (cans, tins, foil)
- 8% – ashes, dust from the vacuum cleaner
- 10% – other

What a waste!

Look at the photos and ask yourself this question. Is it really necessary to produce so much waste?

How long do we use plastic packaging before it is thrown away?

What other sort of container can we get milk in?

Why don't we buy all our drinks in returnable bottles?

What can we do?

Twenty million tonnes of rubbish is a massive amount of rubbish to throw away every year. Some local councils now provide kerbside collection services for collecting domestic waste for recycling. It seems that if recycling is made easy, most people are willing to co-operate.

What can you do? Find out what recycling services are available in your area. Contact the local council and Friends of the Earth.

The three Rs for the environment

Radioactive waste

Some radioactive waste comes from industry and hospitals but most comes from nuclear power stations. It is a serious environmental problem – all we can do is store it. But where? At sea? Deep underground? If it leaks out, will it harm us, or will it harm future generations? Some people tell us that it is safe, but others say there is no such thing as a safe level of radioactivity.

Is radioactivity natural?

Yes it is. It is called background radiation and there are natural 'hotspots' in some areas of the United Kingdom. Radon gas escapes naturally from granite rocks in the south west of England and the Grampian area of Scotland.

Background radiation occurs naturally in some places in the United Kingdom.

Chernobyl power station, USSR, 1986. The nuclear reactor melted down and then exploded. The radiation affected the quality of this photo!

Is radioactive waste safe?

The environmental disaster at Chernobyl on 26 April 1986 has not helped people accept nuclear power as a safe way to generate electricity.

A large area around Chernobyl was soon heavily contaminated by radioactive fallout. Material from the explosion was also carried up into the atmosphere and drifted across Europe.

Fallout from Chernobyl contaminated land all across the north of the British Isles. Ten years later, some sheep farmers have only just been allowed to sell their lamb again.

Most people are afraid of radioactive waste because its effects last for years.

There are three types of radioactive waste that come from nuclear power stations. These are low level, intermediate level and high level. At the moment, all intermediate and high level radioactive wastes have to be held in stores which are run by the government.

✓ Nuclear power

Countries with limited reserves of fossil fuels (see page 38), such as Japan and France, generate most of their electricity at nuclear power stations. They say nuclear power has environmental advantages.

■ It does not release greenhouse gases.

■ It does not create acid rain.

■ One tonne of nuclear fuel produces as much electricity as 150 000 tonnes of coal.

✗ Nuclear power

These are the kinds of questions that people ask:

■ What are we going to do with the intermediate and high level waste?

■ What are the chances of there being another Chernobyl?

■ For how long will the power station still be radioactive when it comes to the end of its life?

■ What should we do with the plutonium that comes from reprocessing fuel rods? (Plutonium can be used for making nuclear weapons.)

Sizewell B is the latest nuclear power station to be built in the UK, and it could be the last.

What can we do?

France cut its release of greenhouse gases by 80 per cent in seven years by generating electricity from nuclear power. This is good news for global warming. But having read about the advantages and disadvantages of nuclear power, do you think this is the way to generate electricity in the future?

What can you do? Find out more about the arguments for and against nuclear power. Try contacting Nuclear Electric (British Fuel), or organisations such as Friends of the Earth or Greenpeace.

Reduce, reuse, recycle

The developed world has become known as a 'throwaway society' which depends on using up materials extracted from the environment and then throwing them away. Cheap plastics, for instance, have made this possible. The developing world, however, has millions of people who try to reuse, repair and recycle materials wherever possible. At the moment, they produce a lot less waste than we do.

These shoes in a Kenyan market have been made from old car tyres.

Can the developed world continue with this 'throwaway' approach? What if the developing world tries to do the same? Resources won't last forever. How long will the supply of oil last if everyone uses it at the rate of the developed world?

The three Rs

Look at the pictures. Think of other ways you could reduce, reuse and recycle.

What is recycled?

The materials most often recycled are glass, paper and metal. Plastics are the hardest to recycle because there are so many different types which can't be mixed and melted down like glass or metal.

Paper

Three million tonnes of paper are recycled each year.

Glass

Half a million tonnes of glass are recycled every year.

Metal

Recycled metal is a profitable business. Aluminium can fetch £600 per tonne.

Plastic

It's estimated that, by the year 2000, more than a billion tonnes of plastic around the world will be thrown away each year.

Clothes

Old clothes can be taken to charities such as Age Concern and Oxfam.

Biodegradable plastics

We can now make plastics which eventually break down when exposed to light for a certain length of time. There are advantages and disadvantages to this. Does it solve any of the problems? Is it a sustainable way of using materials from the environment (see page 6)?

Is recycling always best?

In Thailand, recycling paper has caused problems. It's not the paper that's the problem, but the ink that is removed during recycling – it pollutes the rivers.

Plastic is difficult to recycle but it can be used to make things like T-shirts!

What can you do?

Local Agenda 21

All councils must publish a strategy (plan) for recycling. Ring up or write to your local council to find out how you could get involved (see page 4).

Eco Schools

Contact The Tidy Britain Group to find out more about the Eco Schools Project.

Action Earth

You could join a national project such as Action Earth which could help you meet other people who care about the environment. Ring Community Service Volunteers (CSV Environment).

Fresh water

Providing fresh water for everyone in the 21st Century is not going to be easy. At the moment, a third of the countries around the world don't get enough – even for their basic needs. In the developed countries, things are very different. People expect to get pure, high quality water through their taps whenever they wish. Although the Earth is covered in water, less than 1 per cent is actually fresh. The rest is salt water.

Water in the developing countries

The map (below) shows the countries around the world where fresh water is not so safe to drink. Look at other maps in this book to see where deforestation and desertification are happening (see pages 16 and 20). What do you notice?

In Kenya, the systems for collecting and piping water to the people are very poor. In rural areas, most people have to fetch and carry it.

Global change

We know that industry and the use of the car could be changing the atmospheric environment and affecting weather patterns around the globe. Could global warming be damaging countries which are short of fresh water?

If the Earth warms even by a degree or two, it could upset the pattern of rainfall around the world. Some countries might get more rain and others might get less.

Local change

Could cutting down forests be changing local climates and weather patterns? Rainforests soak up rain like a sponge. Water moves back and forth between the forests and the air. If you cut down the trees, the local climate will almost certainly change. It could also lead to soil erosion and desertification (see page 20).

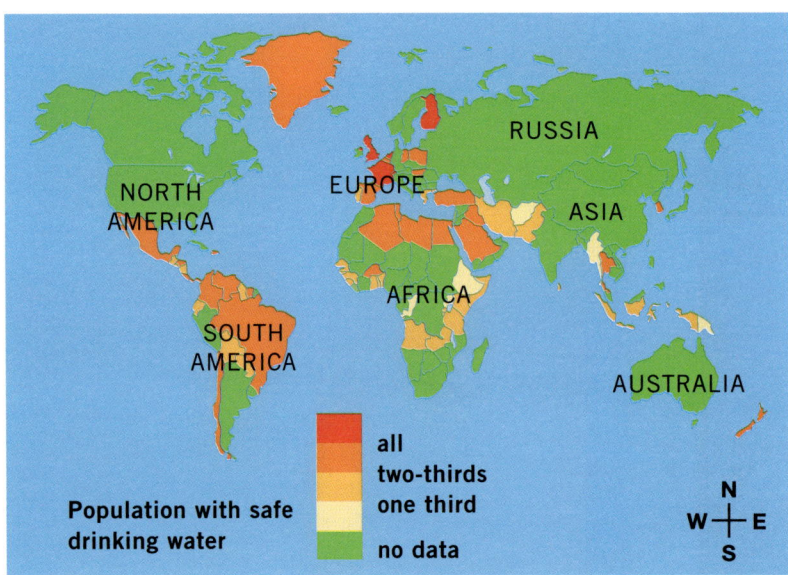

Where are most of the countries where water is not so safe to drink?

Water in the developed countries

People in the developed countries expect pure water to be on tap. The European Union sets standards on quality so that our water is almost 100 per cent pure. It must also be free of microbes. That's why it often smells of chlorine. The demand for more and more water is steadily increasing. Why? The pictures (below) might give you a clue.

It's thought that each person in the developed world uses about 150 litres of water every day, but uses only 3 litres for drinking and cooking. The rest is 'wasted'.

Somehow, we are still not satisfied with our tap water and many of us are now buying bottled water for drinking. Unfortunately, this water comes in plastic containers which immediately creates another environmental problem. Why do you think people buy bottled water?

What can we do?

At the moment, 25 per cent of people on this Earth don't get safe drinking water. Agenda 21 recommends that, by the year 2025, there should be safe water for everyone to use. It's not really possible to transport water around the world, and it's too expensive to take the salt out of seawater (desalination). The most helpful thing we can all do is try to reduce our release of greenhouse gases into the atmosphere.

What can you do? Look at the pictures on this page. Think about how much water is 'wasted'. Perhaps you could change the way you use water.

These pictures show how water is 'wasted'.

Seaworld

The seas around the British Isles are a cheap dumping ground for chemical waste. We dump sewage, chemicals, oil and radioactive waste. But what are we doing to the environment of millions of plant and animal species that live in this underwater world? Do we know what chemicals could be coming back to us through the food chain when we eat animals and plants from the sea?

20% of toxic waste in the North Sea flows from British rivers.

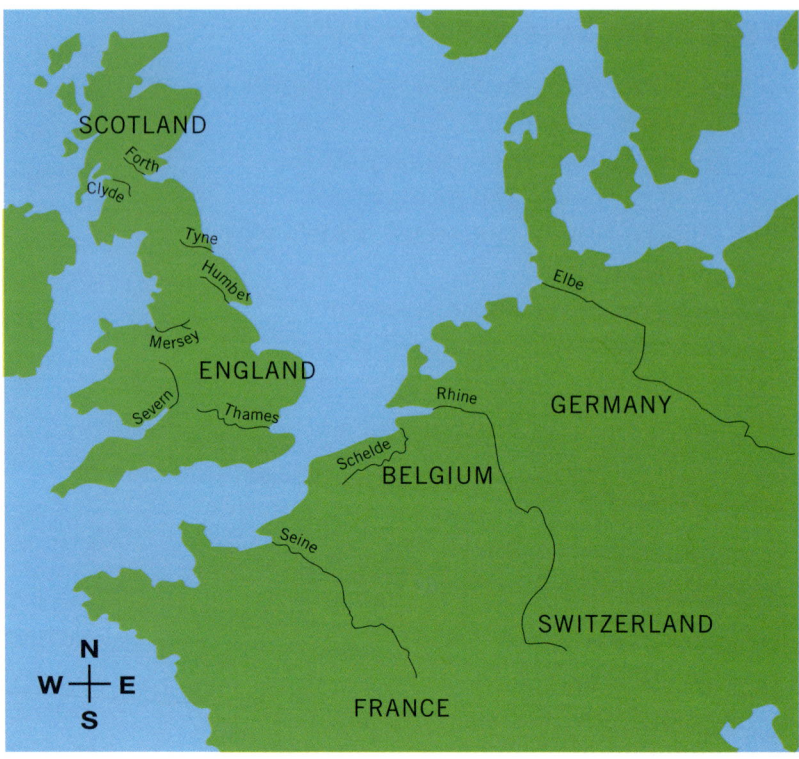

Where is all the waste coming from?

Two million tonnes of toxic (poisonous) waste flow out of the major rivers into the seas around the British Isles. Toxic waste includes fertilisers, pesticides, radioactive material and heavy metals (e.g. lead, mercury). Some of this waste comes from chemical and other industries, but fertilisers and pesticides simply run off farmers' land into the rivers. All these pollutants can get into the food chain, but the most worrying are the fertilisers and pesticides that enter the sea in such large quantities.

Look at the map (above). Why do you think the river Rhine carries more waste than all the others? Notice where it starts.

Some beaches have been awarded the blue flag. This means the water is safe for bathing. What might be wrong with the beaches that are not awarded a blue flag?

This beach in Dyfed, Wales has been awarded the blue flag for being clean and safe.

If the sea becomes cloudy, what might happen to the food chain? Why?

Are we damaging the sea?

People argue that because the sea is so enormous, any waste we tip into it is soon diluted and broken down. Look at the picture above. It shows how sewage sludge could disturb food chains in the sea.

What can we do?

Agenda 21 says we should protect our coastlines from pollution. But this isn't easy. It is already against the law to dump oil at sea, but more oil still comes from ships cleaning their tanks illegally than comes from disasters such as the *Exxon Valdez* or the *Sea Empress* (1996). All we can do is try to reduce our need for oil.

Sewage sludge dumping in the North Sea

Tourism

Have you ever been on a package holiday abroad? It was probably to a place with different people to you and with a different way of life. Package holidays have opened up the world to global travel. This has brought benefits to many poorer countries by bringing in valuable cash, but it has also had a serious effect on their environments. What effect might you be having on other parts of the world when you travel? Are you environmentally responsible?

What's the problem?

By the year 2000, the number of tourists travelling abroad each year will reach 700 million. Tourists want to travel to more and more exotic places which then struggle to cope with the needs of so many extra people. Think about the problems being shown in these photos.

Clearing trees to make ski slopes in the French Alps has created an earthslip.

Vehicle pollution can damage the plant and animal life. The noise can also cause distress to some animals, like the cheetah, who leave their kills uneaten.

Eco tourism

Eco tourism is about trying to keep the balance between the needs of the tourist and the ability of the local environment to cope. If there isn't a balance, then the result will be environmental damage.

Green travel

Some tour operators offer 'green' package holidays which are sensitive to the environment being visited. These tour operators are likely to be members of CERT (Campaign for Environmentally Responsible Tourism). Look for the logo:

Campaign for Environmentally Responsible Tourism

It is also possible to join special environmental research expeditions such as Earthwatch or the British Schools Exploring Society. (You must be over 16.)

Earthwatch is an international science foundation which works to sustain the world's environment, monitor global change and conserve endangered species.

The British Schools Exploring Society involves young people working in remote corners of the world on a range of projects that contribute to our understanding of the environment.

> **What can you do?**
> There are some simple things you can do when you travel abroad on holiday:
>
> ■ Be environmentally sensitive – other countries are not necessarily like yours. Each country has its own environment with different people and a different way of life which should be respected.
>
> ■ Don't buy products made from endangered species (see page 18).
>
> ■ Don't leave litter – if it's plastic, take it back home.
>
> ■ Reduce the amount of water you use – water is scarce and valuable.

Carnival time, Rio de Janeiro. Every country has its own environment and culture which should be respected.

Transport today

In the developed world, the car is a way of life. It is seen as essential for work and for leisure. People enjoy the freedom to get around as and when they like. However, there are environmental costs to be paid. As well as using up non-renewable fuel, cars produce greenhouse gases and poisonous fumes that pollute the air we breathe.

Global effects

Every time you use the car you are adding carbon dioxide to the atmosphere, and contributing to global warming. In the developed world, about 25 per cent of the carbon dioxide comes from traffic. The freedom of the open road is the dream of most motorists, and some people may be lucky enough to find one.

Lots of people experience traffic like this.

A traffic jam in Bangkok. Is this how the future will look?

It's thought, for example, that an average German motorist spends 65 hours a year stuck in traffic jams, and this will double over the next twenty years. But it's not just a problem in the developed world. We are now finding just the same problems in the big cities of the developing world.

Taking your breath away

Although petrol and diesel cars both produce carbon dioxide and other pollutants, it is not clear which of them causes the most pollution.

Breathing in car fumes is hazardous to health. If the cyclist has breathing problems like asthma or bronchitis, then car fumes will make these problems worse. The fumes can also cause other problems such as heart disease and cancer.

Smog in Mexico City

Smog

Chemical reactions involving car fumes are sparked off by bright sunlight and make ozone. At ground level, ozone is extremely poisonous. Where is ozone an important gas?

Are there any solutions?

Some countries in the developed world now have strict standards about pollutants from car exhaust pipes. Some insist that catalytic converters are fitted (see below).

Catalytic converters can only be fitted to cars that run on unleaded fuel, and they only work efficiently when they are fully warmed up. As most journeys are between three and five miles, is the catalytic converter a real solution?

Carving a way forward!

Cars need roads, and roads need space. A new bypass, therefore, makes great changes to people's local environments. Do you agree or disagree with the following statements:

■ New roads cause motorists to make more journeys.

■ Bypasses improve the health of people living in the town.

■ Habitats for wildlife are more important than roads.

■ Bypasses reduce traffic jams.

■ People living in the path of the new road lose their homes, but the local community will benefit.

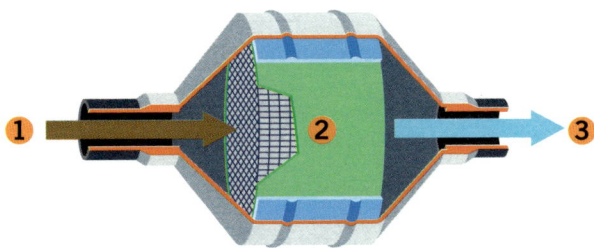

❶ exhaust fumes enter here

❷ nitrogen and sulphur oxides, hydrocarbons and particulates are removed

❸ pollutants are reduced but carbon dioxide is still present

What can we do?
Today, there are 500 million cars worldwide. The motor industry is developing 'lean burn' engines which will use less fuel. But if we drive more miles, we are still pumping greenhouse gases into the air. The easiest solution is for governments to make driving very expensive.

What can you do? Find out what your family and friends think about their cars. Would they give them up or use them less?

Transport tomorrow

Are cars a danger to health, and a threat to the environment through the global warming they cause? How many jobs are involved in building cars and trucks and using them to transport goods? Will people ever give up the personal freedom they get from a car which allows them to go where and when they like? Your answers to these questions could shape the future of your environment.

Tram system, Manchester. Investing in public transport is expensive. Does it encourage drivers to leave their cars at home?

Looking for alternatives

Each of the pictures on this page represents an idea which could reduce carbon dioxide emissions as well as reducing health risks from pollution. What does each picture suggest to you? What are the problems with each idea?

A Park and Ride terminus in Cambridge. People still use their cars to get to the terminus!

If cycling was safer, would you prefer to make your journeys on a bike?

An electric car. Where does electricity that is used to charge the batteries come from?

Private or public transport?

All sorts of vehicles are made from non-renewable resources. These vehicles also use up non-renewable fuels to make them go. They release greenhouse gases which add to global warming, and poisonous gases which damage people's health. They can also cause dreadful congestion.

More cars mean more roads. New roads can destroy people's homes and rare wildlife habitats. They can also encourage people to drive even more. Vehicles can also kill thousands of people every year. With so many disadvantages, why are people so reluctant to give up or reduce the use of their cars?

If you ask motorists why they won't use public transport, they often say:

- There aren't any buses or trains available.
- It's much more expensive.
- It doesn't go where you want to go.
- You have to wait, so it takes longer.
- You have to share and it's not so comfortable.
- You can't carry lots of things.
- The motor industry creates jobs for people.

What can we do?

How could we make public transport more attractive to people in the future? Here are some suggestions for you to think about:

- Build lots of new public transport systems.
- Make it cheap to travel on public transport.
- Make car drivers pay road tolls to drive in urban areas.
- Introduce traffic calming systems to slow traffic right down.
- Only allow electric cars in urban areas.
- Make all city centres for pedestrians and cyclists only.
- Ban private transport from city centres when pollution levels are high.

What can you do? Imagine you are a car driver and still want to use your car, but you feel strongly that you must try to reduce the damage your car has on the environment. These pictures (below) will give you some ideas of what you could do.

Coal, gas and oil

Do you burn coal, gas or oil (fossil fuels) in your home, or use products that are made from them? Most people in industrial countries do. They rely on coal, gas and oil for making electricity, and for producing consumer goods.

Unfortunately, all the processes needed to get coal, gas and oil out of the ground, and the uses we have for them, cause damage to the environment in one way or another. What would be a more sustainable way of using these fossil fuels without damaging the environment?

Look at the pictures and think about the sort of environmental damage that might be happening in each case.

Transporting oil

There are major oil fields around the world. The problem is that once the oil has been extracted from the ground or sea, it has to be transported to oil refineries. This can be done over land by huge pipelines or by sea in massive tankers which carry 120 000 tonnes of oil at a time.

The *Sea Empress* lost over 65 000 tonnes of oil into the UK's Maritime Nature Reserve before it was eventually floated off the rocks.

Oil is not the only cause of environmental damage. Detergent is sprayed on the oil slick to break it up and stop it washing on to the beaches. This spray produces even more toxic chemicals which damage the vital food chains in the sea.

Spoil from a slate mine, Wales. If it rains heavily, what will happen?

Oil lost from the *Sea Empress*, Tenby, Wales

The ocean wastebin

The Brent Spar is the remains of a massive North Sea oil rig. It contains toxic metals, such as lead and mercury, and also hydrocarbons, organic compounds and radioactive drilling fluids.

The Shell Oil Company wanted to dump the Brent Spar in 2000 metres of water, far out in the Atlantic Ocean. It's thought that it takes water from this depth at least 250 years before it returns to the surface. By this time, all the poisons should be broken up. Greenpeace were against dumping the rig. They argued that it should be decontaminated and recycled instead. There are many more rigs still out in the North Sea. How do you think they should be disposed of?

The Brent Spar is towed from the Atlantic into a Norwegian fjord.

Fossil fuel power stations

Burning coal, gas or oil to make electricity produces pollutants such as carbon dioxide, sulphur dioxide and nitrogen oxides. Look at this table:

Power station	CO_2	SO_2	NO_x
Coal	✓	✓	✓
Oil	✓	✓	✗
Gas	✓	✗	✗

Why will all three contribute to global warming? Which types of power stations are likely to produce acid rain?

Consumer goods

Coal and oil are rich raw materials which can be used to manufacture consumer goods such as plastic cups and textiles. Think about the following questions:

■ Why do we burn fossil fuels if they cause global warming?

■ Why do we use them to make throwaway goods?

■ Why are these goods so difficult to get rid of?

■ Why do we burn them if we can make things from them?

■ What will we use when the coal, gas and oil have run out (see pages 40–41)?

What can we do?
We all know that fossil fuels will run out soon, but it doesn't stop us using our cars, central heating, air conditioning or electrical goods. How can we change the attitudes and behaviour of people in the developed countries?

What can you do? Get in contact with your Local Agenda 21 group and find out what you can do to help.

Alternative energy

The developed countries make most of their electricity from fossil fuels and nuclear power. But fossil fuels produce greenhouse gases and acid rain, and nuclear power produces radioactive waste. All of these damage the environment. The search is on, therefore, for other ways of making electricity which do less damage to the environment.

Environment friendly

Are all alternative ways of making electricity friendly to the environment? Ask yourself these questions to decide what the advantages and disadvantages of an alternative are:

■ Will it add to global warming?

■ How much electricity will it generate?

■ How much energy will it take to build it and how expensive will it be to run?

■ What effect will it have on the local environment?

– Will people have to move?

– Will wildlife habitats be destroyed?

– Will it be a blot on the landscape?

■ How long will it last and what will happen to it at the end of its life?

■ Will it produce waste disposal problems?

Use these questions to help you think about the environmental impact of these alternative ways of making electricity. You won't know all the answers but you will get an idea of the problems. Look at the examples on these pages:

Solar cells collect sunlight and use the energy to make electricity.

Wind turbines produce no emissions and have a low running cost.

A hydro-electric power station in Sri Lanka

Hydro-electric power station

A dam holding back billions of litres of water is a massive store of energy which can be used to make electricity. But a dam creates a reservoir, which floods the land behind it and affects the waterflow downstream.

Local people feel strongly about these schemes. Can you think why? Hydro-electric power stations are very expensive. They also cause many environmental changes both during the building process and afterwards. But they don't produce greenhouse gases.

Biomass fuels

Many native people in developing countries get their fuel from wood, charcoal and animal dung. Think about the environmental advantages and disadvantages of using these energy sources.

A tidal barrage. The movement energy in the tides can be used to make electricity, but a massive barrier has to be built to do it.

What can we do?

Electricity is vital in developed countries as high standards of living depend on it. The developing countries also see this as the way to improve their standard of living.

What do you think of the future of fossil fuels and nuclear power for generating electricity? Do you think we should be looking for new sustainable sources of energy?

What can you do? Ring your Local Agenda 21 group for some ideas.

Action taking

Action taking is about your contribution to caring for this planet. For many of you it will be about choosing 'green' (environmentally friendly) products and becoming informed. Action taking depends on how you see the planet being preserved in the future, and how we can provide for the needs of future generations.

Think globally, act locally

You may feel that there is not much you can do on your own about the big issues concerning the environment. Acting locally means that lots of people acting together can make a real difference on a global scale. Through your actions, you can inform others and encourage 'green' actions by lots of other people. Turn to pages 4 and 5 for ideas of how you can get involved locally.

Environmental audit

The point of an environmental audit is to help you to find out how wasteful or efficient you are in the use of resources. You can then take action to reduce the amount of energy, water and other resources which you use and find ways to reduce the level of waste. These actions may not only make you 'greener', but they may save you money as well.

Water

Make a list of all the ways you use water. Here are some ideas:

Water	litres per day
■ making tea/coffee	
■ taking a bath	
■ washing up	
■ flushing the toilet	

Can you think of any others?

You could hold a recycling sale with friends.

Household rubbish

The average household produces 10–15 kg of rubbish per week. It's estimated that 70 per cent of all household rubbish can be recycled. How close can you get to this?

Collect one day's rubbish. Separate and weigh the different types of rubbish. Draw a pie graph or chart to show what's in your waste. Decide what percentage of waste you could recycle if you really wanted to.

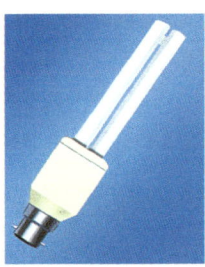

Energy

The way you use electricity and fuel in the home has a direct effect on the environment. The more you use, the more greenhouse gases are released either from your home or at the power station.

Check out your home. Do you have:

	Yes	No
■ draught proofed doors/windows		
■ low energy light bulbs fitted		
■ hot water pipes/tank lagged		
■ thermostatic valves on radiators		
■ loft insulation		
■ plastic double glazing fitted		
■ cavity wall insulation		

As a result of taking action, every unit of electricity (kilowatt hour) you save from your electricity bill can save the power station releasing 1 kg of carbon dioxide.

Travel

How many miles does the family car do each week?

Check out your travel. Make a checklist of journeys and number of miles each day for a week. Here are some ideas:

Journey	Miles
■ trip to school and back	
■ trip to supermarket	
■ trip to football game	

For each journey, think about whether it could be done using another form of transport, such as walking, bicycle, bus, train, or sharing a lift. Decide when you prefer to use the car.

Each litre of petrol releases about 2 kg of carbon dioxide into the atmosphere. Find out how many miles per gallon your car does. (1 gallon = 4.5 litres)

Try making some journeys without the car. Work out how many kilos of carbon are saved from going into the atmosphere.

The future?

Having read about the environment in this book, what kind of future do you want for your children and grandchildren? Do you see a future where people will have respect for each other and for other species? Do you think people will work together for the good of the planet?

The pictures and writing on these pages show some of the problems we face in the future and get you to think about how we can try to change things together.

Third World's lament

The First World has had its fun
The Third World's just begun
But fluorocarbons from the fridge
Make ozone holes we cannot bridge
So poverty must be our lot
And development, it seems, must stop.

They tell us: 'Rice fields pollute more
    than our cars!'
So pressure is put on poor countries
    like ours
For decades of indulgence, they pay
    no price,
But in such matters, we have no rights.

The First World goes all out for their kill
And the poorer nations become
    poorer still.
A change of heart must take place
If the poorer world is to see better days.

Rekha Menon, aged 14, India

Glossary

acid rain   Rain containing acid that comes from gases in the air such as sulphur dioxide

biodiversity   The wide range of species of plants, animals and microbes living on this planet. The word comes from *bio* meaning 'life' and *diversity* meaning 'varied'.

CFC   Short for chloro-fluoro-carbon. It is a man-made gas which breaks up the ozone layer. It is an ODS (see page 47).

climate   The pattern of weather that occurs in a particular part of the world (e.g. rainforests have a tropical climate)

contaminated   Polluted or poisoned

decontaminated   Free from pollution or poisons

deforestation   The clearing of trees and shrubs from the land

desalination   The process that makes fresh water from sea water

desertification   The process by which soil loses its fertility so that it can no longer support the growth of plants

developed countries   The rich and industrialised countries. People in these countries use up high levels of energy and resources.

developing countries   These are not industrialised and are much poorer than the developed countries. They use far lower levels of energy and resources.

ecosystem   The environment in which plants, animals and microbes are linked together by food chains (e.g. a rainforest or the ocean)

emission   The release of gases which pollute the atmosphere

erosion   The wearing away of soil or rock by wind and water

food chain   Who eats what (e.g. we eat animals which have eaten plants)

fossil fuels   Formed along with fossils many millions of years ago (e.g. coal, gas and oil)

global warming   The steady but slight increase in the temperature of the Earth's atmosphere (also known as the 'greenhouse effect')

greenhouse gases   Gases, such as carbon dioxide, that trap the Sun's energy on the surface of the Earth. They are thought to be the cause of global warming.

habitat   Where a group of plants and animals live (e.g. a hedgerow)

hydro-electric power (HEP)   This comes from water falling from a high level (e.g. top of a dam) to a lower level. The energy from falling water is used to drive turbines which then generate electricity.

industrial countries   Rich countries with highly developed technologies which give most of the people a high standard of living

melanoma   Cancer of the skin

nitrogen oxides (NO_x)   Gases emitted from vehicles and industry which pollute the atmosphere

non-renewable resources   These cannot be replaced once they have been used up (e.g. fossil fuels, metals and plastics)

nuclear power   The generation of electricity by the splitting of uranium atoms

ozone depleting substances (ODSs)   These break up the ozone layer (e.g. CFCs and freon)

ozone layer   The delicate layer high in the stratosphere that blocks out harmful radiation from the Sun

pesticides   Chemicals designed to kill insects and other animals which would otherwise destroy crops

photochemical smog   Occurs in towns and cities and is caused by sunlight reacting with vehicle pollution

photosynthesise   When plants make their own food from carbon dioxide and water, using light from the Sun

pollution   The poisoning of air, water or land

radioactivity   Released by radioactive materials as they break down. It can be very harmful.

recycling   Making new things out of materials that would otherwise be thrown away

renewable resources   Can be replaced in a fairly short space of time (e.g. paper or wool)

solar cell   Can use the energy from sunlight to generate electricity

solar radiation   The energy that comes from the Sun

stratosphere   The upper part of the atmosphere where the air is very thin and where the ozone layer can be found

sulphur dioxide (SO_2)   A pollutant gas that is released mainly from coal-fired power stations. It is the main cause of acid rain.

sustainable development   Meeting the needs of people today without damaging the environment for people in the future

tidal barrage   A barrier built across an estuary which uses the energy in the tides to generate electricity

toxin   A poisonous material

United Nations (UN)   The organisation that brings together most of the countries of the world

unsustainable development   A lifestyle that cannot be supported by the Earth's resources

Index

acid rain 2, 3, 8, 12–13, 25, 39, 40, 46
Agenda 21 4–5

biodiversity 2, 4, 17, 18, 19, 46
biosphere 2, 46

carbon dioxide 2, 4, 9, 10–11
  from fossil fuels 39, 43
  from vehicles 34–35, 36
CFCs (chlorofluorocarbons) 2, 8, 11, 14–15, 46
chemicals 30, 38, 40
climate change 4, 9, 11, 28
coal 12–13, 38–39
conservation 5
consumer goods 7, 38–39
crops 8, 19, 20, 21
cycling 36, 37, 43

decontamination 39
deforestation 3, 20–21, 28, 46
desalination 29, 46
desertification 3, 20–21, 28, 46
detergent 38
dioxin 22
drought 10

electricity 2, 13
  environmentally friendly 40–41
  fossil fuel 10, 38–39
  nuclear power 24–25
  for transport 36, 37
  from waste 22
endangered species 2, 9, 18–19, 33
energy, alternative 2, 40–41
energy use 43

environment
  global 2, 5, 8–9
  pollution 7, 19
erosion 17, 20–21, 28, 46

fallout 24
fertilisers 30
flooding 10, 41
food chain 3, 30–31, 38, 46
fuel
  biomass 41
  fossil 2, 10, 25, 38–39, 40–41, 46
  non–renewable 34, 37

gas
  exhaust 12, 34–35
  for fuel and energy 13, 38–39
  methane 11, 22
  radioactive 24
  toxic 2, 12, 37
  see also greenhouse gases
global warming 2, 3, 10, 17, 25, 46
  from fossil fuels 39, 40, 41
  and fresh water 28
  and vehicles 34, 36, 37
greenhouse gases 2, 4, 10–11, 29, 46
  and electricity 40, 41, 43
  from vehicles 34, 35, 37
  and waste 22, 25

habitats 18, 19, 35, 37, 40, 46
homes 17, 19, 22, 37
hunting and poaching 18–19
hydrocarbons 35, 38

incineration 22

industry 3, 12, 37

landfill site 22
landslides 17
logging 17

metals, toxic 38
mining 17, 38

nitrogen oxide 12, 13, 35, 39, 47

oil 6, 26, 30, 31, 38–39
over–grazing 3, 20–21
oxygen 14, 16
ozone 35
ozone depleting substances (ODSs) 15, 47
ozone holes 2, 14–15, 44
ozone layer 2, 8, 14, 47

pesticides 30, 47
plastics 29, 39
  biodegradable 27
  and oil 6, 31
  recycling 26–27
  waste/litter 22–23, 33
plutonium 25
poisons (toxins) 3, 22, 47
pollution
  air 34–35
  atmospheric 12
  environmental 7, 19
  health risks 36
  noise 32
  river/lake 13, 17, 27
  sea 30
  traffic 5, 9, 32, 34–37
  waste 6–7
  water 3, 22

polystyrene 15
population 7, 19
poverty 20, 21, 44
power station 43
  fossil fuel 12–13, 39
  hydro–electric 41
  nuclear 13, 24–25, 40

radiation, background 24
rainforest 2, 11, 16–17, 19, 28
ranching 17
recycling 5, 15, 39, 47
  taking action 42, 43
  waste 22, 23, 26–27
resources 3, 6, 7
rivers and lakes 13, 17, 27

sea 3, 30–31
sewage 30, 31
smog, photochemical 13, 35, 47
soil 3, 13, 17, 20–21, 28
starvation 20, 21
sulphur dioxide 12, 13, 35, 39, 47
sustainable living 6–7

tourism 32–33
traffic jams 34–35
transport 3, 10, 12, 34–37, 43

ultra–violet rays 2, 14, 15

waste 6–7, 27
  chemical 30
  disposal problems 40
  domestic 3, 22–23, 42–43
  radioactive 3, 24–25, 30, 40
water 3, 5, 22, 28–29, 42
weather patterns 10, 28

Published by BBC Educational Publishing
First published 1996
© Keith Bishop/BBC Worldwide (through BBC Education) 1996
The moral right of the author has been asserted.

All rights reserved. No part of this publication may be reproduced, stored in any form or by any means mechanical, electronic, photocopying, recording or otherwise without prior permission of the Publisher.

Paperback ISBN: 0 563 37352 0
Hardback ISBN: 0563 37353 9

Colour reproduction by Dot Gradations, Essex
Colour origination in England by Tinsley Robor, London
Printed and bound by Cambus Litho, East Kilbride

Illustrations: © Maltings Partnership 1996 (pages 7, 10, 12, 16, 20, 22, 24, 28, 30, 31 and 35), © Satchel Illustration 1996 (pages 11, 18. 29, 42, 43 and 44 – 45), © Cathy Morley 1996 (pages 8 – 9)

Photo credits: BBC/Simon Pugh pp. 6 (all), 8 (left), 14 (left, right, bottom), 23 (top, left), 26 (bottom right, middle); Keith Bishop p. 27; CERT p. 32 (bottom right); Bruce Coleman Collection/Frithfoto p. 17; Bruce Coleman Collection/ Steven Kaufman p. 18; Bruce Coleman Collection/Luiz Claudio Marigo p. 33 (bottom); Earthwatch p. 33 (top); EPL/John Arnould p. 9 (bottom); EPL/Bill Barclay p. 13 (top); EPL/Martin Bond pp. 25, 40 (top); EPL/Robert Brook pp. 8 (top), 38 (top); EPL/Nigel Dickinson p. 32 (top); EPL/Neil Dyson p. 36 (middle); EPL/P. Fryer p. 31; EPL/Dylan Garcia p. 23 (bottom); EPL/Herbert Girardet p. 11; EPL/Charlotte MacPherson p. 26 (bottom left); EPL/Michael Marchant p. 36 (left); EPL/John Novis p.41 (bottom); EPL/Trevor Perry p. 5 (right); EPL/Dominic Sansoni p. 41 (top); EPL/Richard Smith p. 15 (main); Friends of the Earth p. 8 (bottom); Going For Green p. 4 (right); Greenpeace Communications/Sims p. 39; ICCE/Jacolyn Wakeford p. 42; Metrolink/Margaret Robinson p. 36 (top); NHPA/Anthony Bannister p. 32 (bottom left); NHPA/David Woodfall pp. 5 (left), 30; Panos Pictures/Jean-Léo Dugast p. 34 (bottom); Panos Pictures/Jasper Young p. 38 (bottom); Planet Earth Pictures/Jonathon Scott p. 19 (bottom left); Premium/Robert Harding Picture Library p. 9 (top); Rex Features p. 24; Science Photo Library/Martin Bond p. 13 (bottom); Science Photo Library/Simon Fraser p. 40 (bottom); Science Photo Library/NASA p. 2; Science Photo Library/NOAA p. 14 (top); Science Photo Library/David Parker p. 34 (top); Science Photo Library/James Stevenson p. 15 (inset); Southern Electric p. 36 (bottom right); Still Pictures/DRA p. 3; Still Pictures/David Drain p. 22; Still Pictures/Mark Edwards pp. 4 (left), 16, 20 (left and right), 21; Still Pictures/Julio Etchart/Reportage p. 35; Still Pictures/Paul Harrison p. 26 (top); Still Pictures/John Maier p. 19 (top); Still Pictures/Alain Pons p. 9 (right); Still Pictures/Jorgen Schytte p. 28 (top); WWF-UK p. 19 (bottom right)

Front cover: Telegraph Colour Library (both)

WAYLAND PUBLISHERS LTD for the bar chart on page 10; LAROUSSE PLC for the poem 'Third World's Lament' by Rekha Menon (page 44) taken from *Rescue Mission Planet Earth* by Children of the World published by Kingfisher. Copyright © Peace Child Charitable Trust 1994.